IN SEARCH OF ME

The Workbook

By: Lynette M Bradshaw

In Search of Me

A Journey to Self-Love, Self-Worth & Purpose

The Workbook

Revised Edition of "The Journey To Uncover The Real Me 2018

By: Lynette M Bradshaw

Restore Her Worth

In Search Of Me-The Workbook ©2018

In Search of Me-The Workbook

Based On The Original Version of The Journey To Uncover The Real Me

Copyright ©2018 by Lynette Marie Bradshaw writing as Lynette M. Bradshaw.

All rights reserved. This book or any portion thereof may not be reproduced or used in any manner whatsoever without the express written permission of the publisher except for the use of brief quotations in a book review. For information, address Restore Her Worth, P.O. BOX 702 Cedar Hill, Tx 75106

www.RestoreHerWorth.com

ISBN-13: 978-0-9962292-4-1   ISBN-10: 0-9962292-4-8

Unless otherwise indicated, word definitions are from Dictionary.com. Copyright © 2015 Dictionary.com, LLC. All rights reserved.

Unless otherwise indicated, Scriptures quoted are from The Holy Bible, King James Version, A Regency Bible from Thomas Nelson Publishers. Copyright ©1990 by Thomas Nelson, Inc. All Rights Reserved. Printed in The United States of America.

Images Copyright © 2018 by Lynette Bradshaw Photography
Editing by: Alana Stone Watkins
Author Images: Lynette Bradshaw Photography 2018

Before you turn the pages, I want you to know you are beginning a transformational, brave journey. Every step we take to heal, grow and elevate in our life, requires movement. You are in ACTIVATION mode as you turn these pages.

I have created a complimentary toolkit for you as a thank you for purchasing, "In Search of Me" and/or In Search of Me-The Workbook as an additional tool for you to listen to as you working out or driving in your car.

Claim your audios here: http://bit.ly/InSearchofMeToolKit

Don't forget to use the hashtags #InSearchofMe2018 and #InSearchofMeNow on social media. I look forward to hearing about what God does in your life after reading, "In Search of Me."

Pick up a copy of In Search of Me: A Journey to Self-Love, Self-Worth and Purpose and Moments of Gratitude Journal at www.Amazon.com or www.RestoreHerWorth.com

Don't forget to leave a review on Amazon!!

Table of Contents

Interlude: What I believe 8

Introduction 11

Chapter 1: The Foundation 13

Chapter 2: The Process 29

Chapter 3: Climb The Stairs 40

Chapter 4: Acknowledge Your Pain 53

Chapter 5: Face The Pain 66

Chapter 6: Release The Pain 82

Chapter 7: Learning to Forgive Others 99

Chapter 8: Choosing To Forgive Yourself 116

Conclusion: 132

About the Author 134

Interlude:

What I believe

I believe as women we have endured a lot. We have learned to do what we have to do and many times more than what we need to do. We have learned to survive, one moment at a time. We have faced life as the crippled athlete rushing into the game without talking to the quarterback or coach as to what our next play is.

I believe our belief system has created some unexpected and unnecessary goals in our lives to be able to prove to ourselves and those around us, that we are strong. We have defined strength based on the definition of those who reared us. We have not taken time to analyze our belief system and examine how it affects how we see ourselves and what we believe about ourselves. By not doing that we have been walking out a system that no longer works for us. I want to encourage you to be willing to analyze the belief system and dig deeper to unfold your current mindset. What are you believing about your story? What part of your story did you get stuck in? How did your belief of what is true, determine for you the best way to live your life?

As you work the process of healing in this workbook, allow yourself to answer these questions for yourself. The questions will push you. I believe it has been easier to live as a victim, than rise up out the ashes of what has happened to us. Yet, I also believe that even in those moments feeling crippled and lost, there is purpose. Even in the moments where we are doing what we must do to survive, there is purpose. Even in the moments where our lives seemed to lack color and played before us as a black and white movie, there was purpose. So now, I believe life can come into color and our eyes can become wide open. In doing so, we can learn to do those things we truly desire to do and be who we are meant to be without feeling as if we are on life support.

In this moment accept your eviction notice from your old hood. You remember Victim-Hood and the residents that dwelled there. Fear, unforgiveness, doubt, inferiority, abandonment, rape, molestation, jealousy and more. As you refuse to remain in a hood that leaves you vulnerable to its elements, you begin the process of taking back your power and I applaud you.

Workbook Terminology

Affirmations

We will have affirmations throughout this workbook. Affirmations are those things we believe or make true. Sadly, we have believed the self- taught and life altering affirmation for us. As you say the affirmations to yourself you will be changing the system of belief about yourself and your life as you begin to repeat the affirmations to yourself. As you go through this study, add in your own affirmations based on the different areas in your life you want to shift or change. Make it personal to you.

Permission Prompt

Each chapter has a prompt for you to respond and reflect on what you are giving yourself permission to do based on the lesson. Take time with this and go deeper than surface level. To give permission is to give authority to do something. So, in this exercise you are giving yourself authority to do or be.

Clear The Space

This exercise requires you to work on an area to remove clutter so you can create an atmosphere of clarity. Each declutter session is 10 minutes

Introduction

Thank you for purchasing this companion Workbook for *"In Search of Me: A Journey to Self-Love, Self-Worth & Purpose.* I believe each of us has a purpose. Sadly, the experiences in our lives have buried our truth and stop us from unveiling the women we really are.

It is my purpose with this workbook to push you. It is my goal to empower you. It is my mission to assist you in digging deeper and being healed. You must do the work in order to reap the benefits. I know you are equipped with everything needed to get you through this process. You are in the process of not only uncovering who you really are, but healing. Yes, to peel back the layers of pain and begin to process what you find, brings healing. Many of us has never considered healing as a possibility for us. We learned to deny, ignore and avoid everything that resembled overcoming what has happened in our life. The subconscious mind never sleeps and even as we sleep, we are reflecting and reliving the painful moments and become restless in our life when we are awake. As I have shared with you, I began my journey in darkness. I started my journey not realizing my journey had begun. Through anger, resentment, rage and lack of clarity. Each step of the journey unveiled truth, the good and the bad of it. Resistance was futile because God was in control, and at the appointed time, God allowed the seeds in me to begin to blossom.

It is time to go deeper. Yes, even deeper than before. God never just deals with the surface only. His healing goes beyond the surface level of our pain and He digs into the sore places in order to birth His purposed creation. The wounds that are scabbed over have an end to their place in your life and that is now. Eventually, bandages lose their grip on the skin as the elements begin to penetrate the adhesive holding it in place. The bandages we have used, are losing their grip in our life. The substitutes we have allowed to numb us are losing the anesthetic effects they have had on your wounds. My search for my dad's love in men over time taught me to pretend and become whomever I felt I needed to be in order to be loved. Over time I became numb as I gave my body as payment for love, which is already given to me in God. As my bandages began to expose the wounds beneath, I felt exposed to the dis-ease rotting away at my soul. My appointed time to remove my mask had come.

This is your time, here and now. This is your journey. This is your story. The appointed time to snatch off your masks and your bandages is now. Your stairs are before you and all you need to do is take a step, steady yourself, trust God and MOVE. I am praying for you not to give up, not to back up and to continue your journey boldly and consistently. God forth and overcome

God Bless

Lynette M Bradshaw

Chapter 1:

The Foundation

There are many things in life that affect our self-worth and how we see ourselves. There is a root to the reason we do not feel worthy. We have not felt worthy because we do not love ourselves. We do not love ourselves because we have missing pieces of what love is. It created cracks in our belief system about what love is and how it shows up in our life.

This chart below can address many of those reasons we are where we are right now emotionally and mentally.

In this moment, how do you see yourself? Check each one that applies or add your own below.

Broken	
Abused	
Abandoned	

IN SEARCH OF ME

Addicted	
Unsure	
Lost	
Angry	
Bitter	
Unforgiven	
Not Enough	
Insignificant	
Dumb	
Foolish	
Cheater	
Confused	
Neglected	
Beautiful	

Ugly	
Unwanted	
Liar	
Naive	
Trustworthy	
Driven	
Hopeless	

Add your own here

As you look back at these adjectives you have checked, what are you feeling right now?

The emotions that come to us when we begin to identify what we really feel and how we see ourselves are real and they must be addressed. To address the root cause of our pain is the only way to begin the process of healing. These are the same emotions we have used sex, shopping, achievements, careers, relationships and more to cover our wounds and not apply the work needed to heal them.

I recognize this. Just like you, I used men, sex, relationships and more to feed the empty place within me that was hungry for love. I felt if I could give my body I would be loved. If I gave all of my thoughts over to these people, they would want me. In turn I paid a price with my self-worth. Love, true love, can never be found searching for it in people and things. It must first be found within you. God always meant for you and me to be loved. He is love. As we search within ourselves for the love we need, we discover that God is love within us, and He is the love that replaces all the substitutes we use to heal.

Taking ownership of what you feel about yourself and how you see yourself is a power move in your life. It is not easy to face our truth, but it is a life changing action that takes us from victim to overcomer.

Now is the time we have go deeper to discover why we feel this way. There is a root to how we see ourselves. As we visually see how we feel about ourselves and how we see ourselves, it can bring up the act and words that planted the seed within our soul.

Write your story below and be as honest as possible with yourself.

Exercise:

In my childhood I felt:

IN SEARCH OF ME

In my family I saw:

```
┌─────────────────────────────────────┐
│                                     │
│                                     │
│                                     │
│                                     │
└─────────────────────────────────────┘
```

In seeing this, I believed this about myself, relationships, love:

```
┌─────────────────────────────────────┐
│                                     │
│                                     │
│                                     │
│                                     │
└─────────────────────────────────────┘
```

I see myself as _____ because:

```
┌─────────────────────────────────────┐
│                                     │
│                                     │
│                                     │
│                                     │
└─────────────────────────────────────┘
```

I believe I am:

[ ]

My life changed when:

[ ]

Breathe…

Getting to the root of our pain and how we see ourselves is not easy. I applaud you for making this step. In this process we are identifying our root causes of pain in order for us to step into healing. The roots will pull you down each time you attempt to disconnect from them when you have not identified them. The root causes of pain show up in our daily lives primarily because they are a secret. All secrets breed darkness because they have an air of silence around them. As you identify your roots you can choose to allow them to be dealt with.

Exercise:

As you begin to get to the roots of your pain, you will begin to unveil why you feel the way you do, the reason you feel you don't deserve certain things or to be treated a particular way. Your journey can steal your voice and your ability to see yourself as deserving of any good thing.

Based on what you identified that you feel currently about yourself, answer the questions below:

I feel I lost my ability to speak when I was (raped, beaten, bullied, rejected, abused, abandoned, etc.)

If you tell someone who you are today, what would you say?

I define who I am based on: (ex. Achievements, relationship)

Do you know who you are without identifying your career? Your relationship status? Using outward things to define who we are, goes hand in hand with insecurity and lack of self-love. As we give power to outward sources to determine if we are good, worthy or loveable we are giving them to ability to take away the very thing we tell ourselves they give us. Let me explain, if you only feel loved, valued and important when you are in a relationship, when and if the relationship has problems or dissolves, the security you feel goes away. If you are only happy when you are achieving goal after goal, you risk being unhappy when the achievement doesn't come when you hoped or doesn't happen at all. In our minds we believe these things have something in them that we lack in ourselves and therefore when we have them, it says we are worth something.

By identifying where we are emotionally and mentally right now, we can begin to see the roadmap of our past that created an image or illusion of who we are. The pain of the past, if not dealt with, will continue to show up in our lives and hide the truth of who we really are from us. Yes, you may be divorced, but that is not who you are. Yes, you have been raped, but you are not a rape victim. Yes, you may be single, but that is not who you are. Yes, daddy may not have been in your life the way he should have been, but you are not abandoned. Yet, it is those same experiences and others that have told us who we are. As you go through this workbook, it is my hope that you will allow yourself the freedom to dig deeper underneath these identifying factors in your life and uncover who you are and have been before life happened.

Breathe…

Mirror Work: Look into your eyes, not just at your face.

Look in your mirror and say (your name) _____ you were always special to me. Then say, "I Am Special." Anything you say after I Am becomes your truth. You are shifting how you see yourself with your words.

In this exercise what you are doing is speaking to yourself to remind yourself that before anyone applied their abuse to you, you were special to yourself and you were okay. Now, look in the mirror. Look into your eyes and repeat. Stay there in this moment, even if it is uncomfortable. You were always special. You are special. NO matter the experiences that brought you to this moment, you are special.

How does it feel looking into your eyes and saying this affirmation to yourself?

Normally when looking in the mirror, we are preparing our hair and clothes. Somehow we miss our eyes. I mean really looking into them and seeing what is there. Our eyes tell our truth. Until you are ready to face what is hiding behind them, you will avoid them. By doing the Mirror Work, you are shifting from hiding to being seen, by you. I'm proud of you. Don't run away from this moment. Don't turn your eyes away. Stay there for just a moment and allow yourself to feel what you are feeling. Allow yourself to really see you for who you are after saying this affirmation to yourself.

After you have dealt with the foundation of how you came to where you are right now, it is time to peel back more layers. The process of healing is just that, a process. Each step is valuable. The foundation step is powerful because just like with a house, if the foundation is cracked or unstable, the house will eventually fall over. As you go through this journey, you are restructuring your foundation. You are fixing all the cracks in your life. You are going back into the past and disturbing the foundation and in doing so, you are stirring up the pain, the judgement and the fear that came with everything you have endured.

In chapter 8 of *In Search of Me*, I talked about how the process requires you to look back, evaluate and explore what is behind you that brought you to this moment. In doing so it allows you to move forward. The problem is we get stuck in looking back and we don't move forward because we are judging ourselves, beating ourselves up because of our choices and we simply cannot get past the pain of the wound we uncover.

Yet, in doing the exercise that ask you, "Who are you, really?" it allows you to go through the process by starting with your foundation. Your foundation holds secrets, clues and answers to assist you in later answering the question, "Who Am I?" without defining yourself based on those painful moments in your story.

Exercise:

Clear The Space

You have done lots of work today. I find it easier to think and create when my space is clear and clean. Our home, car or workspace is a reflection on what we feel inside. So, I want you to find one small area (your purse, drawer, etc.) and clear the space, i.e. clean the clutter. Throw away what you have not used in 2 months, if you are able. Throw away visible trash and organize the space. The reason we are working on small spaces, is so you don't become overwhelmed in the process. Set a timer for 10 minutes and clean/remove those things that you no longer have need of. This is a self-love act. You cannot move forward when you have a lot of old things hanging around. The physical act is symbolizing the work you are doing in your heart, mind and soul.

When you are done, document it here:

I cleaned _____ on _____, 20 _____ and I feel

```
┌─────────────────────────────────────────┐
│                                         │
│                                         │
│                                         │
│                                         │
└─────────────────────────────────────────┘
```

The next step is permission. As you uncover parts of yourself that have been hidden, you must give yourself permission to acknowledge, face and deal with what you find. Please complete the Permission Exercise Below.

I give myself permission to: _____ at this stage of my journey to:

In the space below write a letter to yourself about what you are going to give yourself permission to do regarding your foundation. How will your life be different by giving yourself permission to be and do at this stage of your journey to healing?

Breathe…

Prayer:

God thank you for giving me the strength to face my foundation and define how I see myself daily through my eyes. Father, help me to see myself through you and help me to not ignore what I discover and uncover about my foundation. In Jesus name, Amen.

NOTES:

Chapter 2:

The Process

Process is defined as, the action of going forward. Going forward requires looking back, evaluating and exploring what is behind you in your past. In doing so, you can begin to answer many questions you may have about where you in your life now emotionally, mentally and physically. Process is constant. It will always be necessary. Otherwise we become stagnant and unfruitful in your life.

You have identified the foundation of your pain and dysfunction. Please remember this is your life. This is not a race so take your time with step in this process of healing. You are finding the courage to look your past in the eye. Now what? What do you do now? You begin to build and rebuild the places within you, the places you may not have visited since the moment you were hurt. You have closed the door and locked it, shutting the pain inside. In this stage of the journey, which is what you are on, those doors must be unlocked and opened.

Breathe…

Exercise:

When I think about evaluating my past, I feel?

```
┌─────────────────────────────────────┐
│                                     │
│                                     │
│                                     │
│                                     │
└─────────────────────────────────────┘
```

The scariest part about facing my past is?

```
┌─────────────────────────────────────┐
│                                     │
│                                     │
│                                     │
│                                     │
└─────────────────────────────────────┘
```

For many, including myself, evaluating where you started can be paralyzing. The thought of reliving and re-feeling what caused you to lose your voice, your identity, your self-esteem can be paralyzing. You can become hopeless, fearful, to the point is unbearable to face it.

Looking at your foundation is required in order to see what is out of shape, has cracks, is hidden and locked away. The greatest part of this journey is, you are not alone. Had God known you were not ready for this part of journey, you would not be here. Fear may be telling you contrary right now, but trust you are right where you are supposed to by. It is in this stage you begin to snatch off the bandages and the masks in order to get real with yourself.

Exercise:

What have you been using as bandages and masks in your life?

When using physical things/people to be bandages over your wounds, how did this make you feel when looking at yourself in the mirror?

Breathe...

Moving forward to heal requires sacrifice. We can become comfortable with disfunction. We can run from peace because it makes us uncomfortable. You will need to make some sacrifices and release those things that keep you stuck in the cesspool of pain in order for you to have the capacity to receive anything new. The need to run to food, shopping, obtaining another achievement, reaching another milestone in order to feel you are worthy, having sex with men only to feel more worthless afterwards must be sacrificed. These substitutes cannot go with you. They will take up too much room in your mind, will, emotions, heart and soul. They require a lot of energy. They have become your mask. They have covered, or you thought so, your insecurities, your jealousy and your need to be loved. These substitutes have been close companions to you. They allowed you to function, even if in dysfunction. Being comfortable with dysfunction is easy when you don't know any better. God is shaking up your foundation so you can thrive in your life and be the best version of who you are.

We can begin to inflict pain on ourselves by allowing others to abuse us in how they disrespect us. Yes, you can become a self-abuser. You do so when you realize you are being disrespected with words and actions, but you make a decision to stay out of fear you will be alone. You can become a contributor to your wounds. The process stage will pull back the bandages covering your wounded flesh so you can face the truth that is there including the part you contributed to.

Exercise:

When I think about being a part of my pain, I feel?

I am willing to sacrifice_____ or I am not willing to sacrifice_____ In order to heal. Why?

Letting go things and certain people to heal makes me feel?

Breathe...

Inhale what you are doing for yourself right now. Yes, you are taking back your power. You are facing what you may have run from many times and allowing yourself to go through the process. You are beginning to own your truth about yourself and your past and you are moving forward. I am proud of you and you should be also. Give yourself a hug for not giving up on YOU. You deserve it.

In this moment, what thoughts are going through your mind about your past and future?

The hardest part about letting go is?

Mirror Work: Look into your eyes, not just at your face.

Look in your mirror and say (your name) _____ I am strong enough to face my past and heal.

You have begun to open the doors of the past and face the trauma behind the doors you locked away. Now, you are affirming your strength to face it.

How does it feel looking into your eyes and saying this affirmation to yourself?

Exercise:

Clear The Space

You have done lots of work today. I find it easier to think and create when my space is clear and clean. Today, we are doing a mental cleansing. Find a quiet space. Grab a piece of paper and a pen. Set a timer for 10 minutes and write down all the negative thoughts that are in your mind right now after going through this lesson. Try to not think about what you are writing, simply write. When the timer goes off, take the paper, ball it up and burn it. That's right burn it. This is symbolizing the negative thoughts you are placing on the altar and burning them. You are sacrificing your negative thoughts and gaining the capacity to receive new thoughts. You cannot move forward when you have a lot of old things hanging around. The physical act is symbolizing the work you are doing in your heart, mind and soul.

When you are done, document it here:

I cleaned _____ on _____, 20 ____ and I feel

The next step is permission. As you uncover parts of yourself that have been hidden, you must give yourself permission to acknowledge, face and deal with what you find. Please complete the Permission Exercise Below.

I give myself permission to: _____ at this stage of my journey to:

In the space below write a letter to yourself about what you are going to give yourself permission to do regarding your foundation. How will your life be different by giving yourself permission to be and do at this stage of your journey to healing?

Breathe…

Prayer:

God, thank you for giving me the strength to open the doors of my past and not run away. Thank you for helping me go through the process of healing. In Jesus name, amen

NOTES:

Chapter 3:

Climb The Stairs

As we begin the journey to healing, we must be willing to do the work. You have begun to dig up old things, pull down some cobwebs and open your mind to what is possible for your future. For each of us, we walk a different journey because our journeys are so different. Some are the same, but they have shown up in our lives differently and we have responded to them differently. So, don't look at your sister and allow jealousy to rise up in your heart because you perceive she is further along than you. In this section, we are changing our appetite by shifting our thought process, what we accept as ok and honestly take steps daily to rebuild our foundation.

Wholeness and healing will not always feel easy. In fact, it will be painful. Moving forward will always require a shift in mindset, perspective and attitude. That's right even in our attitude about change, we must shift. The idea to change things about us that we have become comfortable with. Now, it's time to climb the stairs to possibilities, healing, freedom and the greater part of you.

As we acknowledge the pain that is holding us in place, we have to ask ourselves questions.

Exercise:

As you acknowledge the pain, what do you believe is holding you in place now?

Do believe you are worthy enough to heal from the traumatic thing you have gone through?

What are you *"Really"* afraid of, right now?

Do you believe you deserve to live free of your past?

Breathe...

Everything in your life right now maybe showing you, that nothing is changing. Even within yourself, you may be questioning if this journey is worth it. These are normal responses when you begin the process of *uncovering who you are, really.* Is it your mind's way to telling you, the old thoughts are still there? There is a battle in the mind that you will have to fight in order to climb the stairs to the light above you. The light is God's love, God's truth and God's hand reaching out to you. He is calling you out of the darkness the pain has enslaved you in.

Not to know what love is, is one thing, but not to know how to love yourself is painful. Fear is paralyzing and it can be one reason why we choose to live the lie we've constructed as life. The desire to know who we are deep within must outweigh the fear of taking a step towards our future. If our minds can remain in fear and doubt we can stay paralyzed. You are never meant to be stagnant in anything that concerns you.

Do you know what love is?

Exercise:

What is love to you? Describe it in your own words…

IN SEARCH OF ME

Do you believe your definition of love, is God's definition of love for you?

Do you apply your definition of love to yourself or God's definition of love?

Who helped to form your definition of love?

Has the definition of love you live by helped you or harmed you?

Breathe…

As you climb the stairs toward wholeness and healing it is a must to challenge what you know, understand and how you apply love. When we have endured abandonment, abuse (mental, emotional, physical and even financially), feeling that you are not enough, feeling insignificant, feeling alone, being raped, being molested, being betrayed, being unheard, being bullied, it changes our image of love for and from others and love for ourselves. Love is something God always meant for us to have. Love was to be known first through our parents. They were our first examples of love, protection, and forgiveness to give us the foundation God meant for us. But what if they didn't have an example? What if they weren't protected? Unknowingly they continued the cycle in you.

In order to break those cycles, you must challenge what you know as truth, love, mentality, belief and more in order to find out who you are underneath what was planted inside you. You took a step when you realized you are not where you want to be in your life. You took another step when you acknowledged you are broken and hurting. Now you are taking another step to challenge how love has shown up in your life in a dysfunctional way.

Exercise:

In what way have you searched for love?

Have you pretended to be something or someone you are not, to receive love?

Breathe…

Each step and choice you made in order to be loved brought you to this moment. As you identify your understanding of love, you can begin to understand your willingness to do whatever and become whomever you need to in order to have what you deemed as love, if only temporarily. The things we accept to show ourselves we are worthy and loveable show us if we are stable in self-love or needy of self-love. A lack of self-love shows up as low self-esteem, low self-worth, low self-dignity, anger, bitterness, obsession and more. It gives us a false understanding of who we are. It creates a hunger and thirst for what we are missing and pushes us to seek after what we feel has skipped us.

Here is something I want you to do:

Find one scripture that tells you how God feels about you and read it. As you read, close your eyes and put your name in the front of the scripture to make it personal and repeat it for 2-3 minutes for 21 days. It takes 21 days to create a new habit, so why not start with a personal one to build up your inner self. For example: *Jeremiah 1:5 says, Before I formed you in the womb I knew you, before you were born I sanctified (set apart) you.* Now you make it personal, _____Before I was formed in the womb, God knew me and set me apart, Amen

You are loved by God and loved so much that He set you apart from everything else and everyone else. If you were the only daughter on earth, He sees you as special enough to set you apart from or sanctified you. This means he deemed you worthy and holy. Your wounds are blocking you from seeing your truth and as God heals them, you will begin to see yourself as loved, wanted and adored.

Mirror Work:

Look into your eyes, not just at your face. Look in your mirror and say (your name) _____ I am loved by God and I love Me, Amen

You have begun to open the doors of the past, address the impact it has had on your ability to love yourself, see yourself as worthy. Now, you are affirming you have always been loved by God. Your affirmation today is powerful and will allow you to eventually look yourself in the eyes and boldly say, "I Am Loved and I Love Me."

How does it feel looking into your eyes and saying this affirmation to yourself?

Breathe...

Exercise:

Clear The Space

You have done lots of work today. I find it easier to think and create when my space is clear and clean. Today, we are doing a mental cleansing. Find a quiet space. Grab a piece of paper and a pen. Set a timer for 10 minutes and write down all the negative thoughts you have about love right now after going through this lesson. Try to not think about what you are writing, simply write. When the timer goes off, take the paper, ball it up and burn it. That's right burn it. This is symbolizing the negative thoughts you are placing on the altar and burning them. You are sacrificing your negative thoughts and understanding about love and gaining the capacity to receive new thoughts and emotions pertaining to loving yourself and receiving God's love. You cannot move forward when you have a lot of old things hanging around. The physical act is symbolizing the work you are doing in your heart, mind and soul.

When you are done, document it here:

I cleaned _____ on _____, 20 ____ and I feel

```
┌─────────────────────────────────────────┐
│                                         │
│                                         │
│                                         │
│                                         │
└─────────────────────────────────────────┘
```

The next step is permission. As you uncover parts of yourself that have been hidden, you must give yourself permission to acknowledge, face and deal with what you find. Please complete the Permission Exercise Below.

I give myself permission to: _____ at this stage of my journey:

In the space below write a letter to yourself about what you are going to give yourself permission to do regarding your loving yourself and accepting God's love. How will your life be different by giving yourself permission to allow God's love to redefine to you what love really is.

Example: I give myself permission to believe I am loved and I was always meant to be loved. As I do this, I will love myself more each day, one moment at a time.

Breathe…

Affirmation: I Am brave enough to take another step for my healing.

Prayer:

God, thank you for healing my understanding of what love is. Thank you for loving me before I was formed inside my mother. I ask you, God, to help me to release my understanding of love that aren't true and embrace your definition of love. I believe love has not skipped me. In Jesus name, Amen

NOTES:

Chapter 4:

Acknowledge Your Pain

The masks we wear or have worn to get us through the day have been used to cover us so no one would know we are broken in spirit, heart and mind. Pain is deafening. Abandonment makes us hold to people whom we should release but we hold on with desperation so we won't feel that feeling of being abandoned again. We can't heal what we are not willing to face. Are you angry? Are you depressed? Are you bitter? You deserve to be free from it all. You deserve to be free no matter what has happened. First you must acknowledge pain even exist in your life in order to allow yourself to feel. Choosing to feel the pain, shines light on it. Shining light on it is acknowledging it exist for you. The places you shine light have been in darkness and when you acknowledge what is there, darkness loses its' power in your life, moment by moment.

Exercise:

Are you angry? Why? With whom?

```
┌─────────────────────────────────────┐
│                                     │
│                                     │
│                                     │
│                                     │
└─────────────────────────────────────┘
```

Are you depressed? Why? About what?

```
┌─────────────────────────────────────┐
│                                     │
│                                     │
│                                     │
│                                     │
└─────────────────────────────────────┘
```

Are you feeling alone? Why?

```
┌─────────────────────────────────────┐
│                                     │
│                                     │
│                                     │
│                                     │
└─────────────────────────────────────┘
```

The things you are carrying as baggage in your mind, emotions and soul has kept you heavy. Not acknowledging it has kept you in denial. Not only are you stuck at your moment of pain but you lack the ability to untie your hands and feet from the pain. Just like an actress has to take off her makeup after a performance. Just like she looks in the mirror and applies the makeup remover to take off everything that created her character for the part she is playing, so do you. It is time to take off the covering you use daily to perform for those around you. Acknowledging the emotions, you feel inside may not feel good, but it is necessary. In the exercise above you answered the questions to some of those emotions. Let's go deeper.

Exercise:

The anger Is attached to what you haven't acknowledged. What action/words done/said to you, do you need to acknowledge?

The feeling of being abandoned, feeling unwanted, feeling you are not enough, feeling you won't ever be anything, etc. Began when?

I try to out run my pain by: (Seeking what I need in others, shopping, sex, etc.)

Breathe…

There are times, we cannot face the pain on our own. As you are bringing the baggage to the surface, it may require you to seek help in professionals (counselors, psychiatrists, Doctors). Don't be embarrassed or afraid to do so. Reaching out for assistance in dealing with what you have acknowledged as pain in your life is a power move. Sometimes we try and carry so much on our own. Truth is, we cannot carry everything on our own. Even though we know God is our help, He has placed unique individuals trained to deal with our unique pain, to help us.

I came to a point in my life where I needed those unique individuals to assist me. The rage I felt as I began to realize something was changing within me was too much and required me to seek help. My counselor was a God send. She helped me to get to the root of the rage. She taught me how to allow the vomit of the pain to come up and deal with it. Sounds awful right? Quite the contrary. We have learned to swallow the stench of pain when it tries to raise its head to let us know it is there. We have been taught and we learned own way of dealing with the stomach pain that represents the wounds of our past. I learned my rage came from frustration. My frustration came from not understanding what I was feeling and why. Why questions were coming from the stirring in my spirit that I could no longer hide my wounds because they were escaping the bandages I had used for over 40 years in order to have some sense of life. When God impressed upon my heart I needed help, I resisted because I was reminded that as a child there wasn't anyone to listen to the little girl in pain. I was reminded no one in my family ever went to counselors, we were supposed to go to God or just shut up. Still, I trusted the unction in my spirit and made the appointment.

I believe to this day, had I not sought outside help, I would no longer be alive on this earth. The deep well of darkness I felt within had begun to engulf me. My marriage had begun to suffocate me. My masks were no longer covering my pain and sadly they never were. One of the things I discovered as my mask and walls began to fall, was that I was depressed, not sad, depressed. Yes, as a Christian woman I faced depression. I also faced thoughts of suicide. Talk about telling secrets, right. I believe we hold so many secret wounds that to me depression is anger turned inward. I had learned to bottle everything up in a nice little package, mold myself into whatever was needed to have attention. Our secrets won't stay secret forever. They ooze into our character and overtake our truth.

Maybe in your home as a child, you heard the saying, "Whatever happens in this house, stays in this house." Sound familiar? Each time you were told to be silent, not to tell how you felt, ignore what you felt, deny anything was done, you lost another part of your voice. So, as you are acknowledging your pain and shining light on it, you can no longer hold on to that old tradition of being silent to protect other people. You must now shine light on the dark places to heal yourself.

Exercise:

How were painful moments addressed in your home as a child?

What secrets are you holding on to from childhood that are suffocating you from within?

Have you turned your rage inward and now you hate yourself because of what you have been through?

[ ]

Why are you afraid of losing by sharing your story with someone who can help you?

[ ]

Breathe...

As you are acknowledging what has been hidden you are stirring up your foundation even more. You are breaking the cycles in your life past down to you from your grandmother, aunts and mom. They gave you what they knew because no one ever challenged what they were given. You, on the other hand, have the opportunity to unmask yourself. You can live in your truth and refuse to allow secret abuse, secret yearnings to be loved, secret earth-shaking words spoken to you by those who said they loved you within your home and in relationships to continue to silence you. You are breaking free.

Mirror Work:

Look into your eyes, not just at your face.

Today we are approaching your mirror work a little different. Many times, when we attempt to look ourselves in the eye in the mirror, the flashes of our past, what we really think about ourselves, overshadows us and we turn away. Today, allow your Mirror Work to be simply, sit and look in your eyes. Do pick and poke at the flaws you may see. Simply sit in quiet. Perhaps turn on your favorite worship or jazz music and sit with yourself. Set your timer for 5 minutes. Settle yourself in your seat and look into your eyes. Allow whatever feelings need to come up and sit with them. Allow yourself to feel and breathe. You will feel uncomfortable but stay there. Don't say a word unless you are praying to God, but the ultimate goal of this exercise is that you become ok with sitting in your stuff, sitting in your silence and seeing your eyes and reconnecting with who you are. I believe in you and I know you will get through this exercise.

Breathe…

Exercise:

What was the hardest part about doing this exercise for you?

What memories, thoughts and feelings came to you while doing this exercise? How do you feel about yourself and the secrets you have been holding?

Be still with what you are carrying within. Don't shy away from it. It will always be with you in one way or another. Yet, as you do the work to acknowledge, shift and release, the power the pain held over you will lessen.

Give yourself a HUG…

No Clutter Exercise today. Take some time and sit with all that you have cleared mentally and emotionally today and allow this to be enough clutter removal today.

The next step is permission. As you uncover parts of yourself that have been hidden, you must give yourself permission to acknowledge, face and deal with what you find. Please complete the Permission Exercise Below.

I give myself permission to: _____ at this stage of my journey:

In the space below write a letter to yourself about what you are going to give yourself permission to do regarding acknowledging your pain, sitting with it and seeing yourself in the mirror. How will your life be different by giving yourself permission to acknowledge what you have hidden for so long?

Example: I give myself permission to no longer run from my silence or my hidden wounds.

Breathe...

Affirmation: I am strong enough to acknowledge what I have kept secret from others and myself in order to walk in wholeness.

Prayer:

God, thank you for giving me the strength to sit with my baggage and acknowledge it. I am grateful to you for being here with me in this process. I trust you more than my pain. In Jesus name, Amen

NOTES:

Chapter 5:

Face The Pain

Now that you have acknowledged your inner pain you must choose to deal with it and not deny it to yourself any longer. When you deal with it, you are facing it. You are facing fear head on and saying, "No More." The masks were to cover the wounds from the pain. The masks begin to crack when we acknowledge the pain. They begin to fall when we face it.

You have lived life wounded thus far because you have tried to run away from that which caused your soul to ball into a fetal position. In order to discover who you are behind the mask, one has to find a morsel of strength, take a deep breath and face the open wounds of their soul.

I longed to be loved, protected, appreciated and wanted. My attitude, my personality, my anger, my up and down ways were the results of being needy of love. I used anger as my defense so no one would hurt me, yet I desperately wanted them to like me.

Exercise:

What pain from your past have you acknowledged and you are ready to face?

What emotions and thoughts are attached to the pain, trauma, abuse, etc?

As a result of these moments in your past, what defense have you been using? Anger? Overachiever? Bitterness?

[   ]

Breathe...

Take a moment and look back at what you just wrote. If you skipped this exercise go back and do it. It is not easy, I know, but by writing out the things we have been running from, it allows us to physically see it. It is not real to us in the natural as it was in our mind, heart and spirit.

As you explore the emotions attached to the pain, trauma and wounds, you will find that anger, fear, insecurity were the results of what you feel has been withheld from you. When we are needy, it shows up in every area of life. When we are needy, it is because there is something that God said belongs to us, is rightfully ours and yet those around us did not have the capacity to give it. We didn't know or understand we were missing something and yet we acted out when it wasn't received.

For example, my need for love ignited a hunger in me to find it. My need to be affirmed, ignited a hunger to do whatever I could to be told I did a good job. The sad thing is, we go outside ourselves searching for these needs and we must begin within ourselves. The root is within. What we need is within. The answer is God. God is love. God has affirmed us. God has accepted us. He lives within and that is where we must begin to fill the emotional, mental, and spiritual voids in our life.

Exercise:

As a result of facing these emotions and situations, what do you think about yourself?

Do you believe because you have experienced trauma and/or abuse, that you are not worthy to be loved? Why?

Do you believe you are worthy of good things after going through what you have gone through? Why?

In this moment, who do you believe you are?

When bringing back to focus those things that make us feel sad, angry, abused, needy, abandoned, etc., they can begin to show us ourselves as the person who went through all the abuse. We become blinded to the truth of who we are at our core and only see ourselves as the abused, the raped, the molested, the victim. Now, it is time to shift your idea of who you are based on what you endured. Yes, these things happened to you. Yes, you feel some sort of way about it, but it is not who you are.

Let me show you this...

I was raised in a home with both parents...Yet I felt unwanted

I was raised in a home with both parents...Yet I felt abandoned

I was raised in a home with both parents...Yet I felt unloved

I was raised in a home with both parents...Yet I felt unworthy

For many years this and more was my identity. I identified myself in every relationship. I showed up in my life identified as the "Un". I parented as the UN. I loved as the UN. These titles became me and I became them. I could not see myself beyond them. They were my tagline. They were my determining factor in everything that involved me. With God's love and many aha moments, I discovered this is not my identity. It is what I experienced and through those experiences I felt I didn't receive what would make me whole. I also discovered I was the perfect person God allowed to walk through this battle. In order to walk into my purpose, I needed to experience *all* of those *un's*. Without them, I couldn't be the woman who helps women walk through their own mental and emotional prison doors in their life. I couldn't know how to change my mindset from Victim to Power HOUSE and teach others to do the same. My journey has been painful but purposeful.

Now you have to decide if your *un's* will continue to be your billboard message or the stone on which you stand. You may have been sexually abused in some way. You may have been physically, mentally or emotionally abused. Your dad may not have been present or present but emotionally disconnected. All these maybe's can be your story but they no longer have to be the deciding factor of how you show up in your life, how you parent, love or believe in yourself. You decide.

Exercise:

Do you believe in this moment that it is possible for you to face your pain and no longer allow it to control you?

Growing up what were UN's in your life? Unloved, Unworthy, Abandoned, Molested

By Facing these things and allowing God to heal you, how can you show differently in your relationships, parenting, etc.?

IN SEARCH OF ME

[ ]

Write the names of the people who planted the seeds of pain in you.

[ ]

What does seeing their names bring up inside of you?

[ ]

Are you ready to release them and the pain they caused? If so, what steps are you willing to take to take back your power from them through the pain they caused?

Breathe…

The desire to be real with yourself and to own your truth has brought you here. You are in a position to be free from the past demons that haunt you today. The steps you are taking is allowing you to give birth to the Real You that has been hidden on the mounds of pain. Each time you wanted to be free, the faces of the names you wrote came before you and you crouched down in fear and anger. No more. Don't back up. Don't be afraid. Face the faces and face the wounds and continue the work to heal yourself in mind, heart, emotions and belief in yourself.

Mirror Work:

Look into your eyes, not just at your face.

As you look into your eyes you are remembering all the work you just completed. You have written down the names of the people who brought pain into your life and faced the demons of the pain. Today you are going to begin to speak to them by name and declare they no longer have power of you.

For example: _____ you made me feel nasty when you _____ to me, but today you no longer have power over me. I am facing the feelings of _____ that you caused me to feel and from this day forward your actions, your words, your intentions will no longer control me. In Jesus' name, Amen

This is not easy, but *you are built for this* and you will get through it. Take some time here. Write it out first if you need to but do it for you. It's time to change your vision about you and in doing these exercises you give yourself tools to shift your life.

Breathe...

Exercise:

What was the hardest part about doing this exercise for you?

[ ]

What memories, thoughts and feelings came to you while doing this exercise? How do you feel about yourself and the secrets you have been holding?

[ ]

Give yourself a *hug*.

Pat yourself on the *back*.

Be proud of *yourself*.

You are doing this. You are still standing. Applaud yourself for finding the courage to look pain in the face and not run away. I'm Proud of You.

Exercise:

Clear The Space

You have done lots of work today. I find it easier to think and create when my space is clear and clean. Today, we are doing a mental cleansing. Find a quiet space. Grab a piece of paper and a pen. Set a timer for 5 minutes and write down all painful emotions and the person who caused them on a piece of paper. Go back to your list in this chapter. Try to not think about what you are writing, simply write. When the timer goes off, take the paper, ball it up and burn it. That's right burn it. This is symbolizing the negative thoughts you are placing on the altar and burning them. You are sacrificing your negative emotions, pain and the images of the people who caused them on the altar. You cannot move forward when you have a lot of old things hanging around. The physical act is symbolizing the work you are doing in your heart, mind and soul.

When you are done, document it here:

I cleaned _____ on _____, 20 ____ and I feel

The next step is permission. As you uncover parts of yourself that have been hidden, you must give yourself permission to acknowledge, face and deal with what you find. Please complete the Permission Exercise Below.

I give myself permission to: _____ at this stage of my journey:

In the space below write a letter to yourself about what you are going to give yourself permission to do regarding facing the pain and acknowledging those who caused it. How will your life be different for you as you continue to work through this process of facing and letting go pain?

Breathe...

Affirmation: I Am stronger than my pain and brave enough to face it.

Prayer:

God, thank you for giving me the courage and faith to face what has been hidden within me. Thank you for allowing me to remember the faces of those who caused me to be in pain and not run away. Thank you for being with me on this journey. I need you as I continue to heal and grow. In Jesus' name, Amen

NOTES:

Chapter 6:

Release The Pain

The root of the pain has been brought to your attention. All the many years of asking and wondering who you were has brought you to this place of getting to the root of the pain. It is not enough to admit you were hurt and acknowledging that there has been pain. The pain must be released.

Our desire to know who we really are opened up those scabbed over wounds.

Exercise:

Is it harder for you to release the pain or the person who caused it?

Breathe…

Most of the pain I dealt with started in my home as a child. So who was in my home? My parents and siblings. My need and hunger for love, my hunger to be seen, my need to be affirmed, began in the place that should have been my safe place. In order to heal those deep wounds, I needed to start at the beginning. I believe it took me longer to release many things because I held on to the people who caused the dysfunction in the early years of my life. As I began to go deeper in my desire to heal, I had to accept the truth God gave me. I had to accept the truth that my parents were taught a certain way and loved a certain way, and they gave the same to me. I had to accept they gave me what they received even though it created inner wounds that would take many, many years to heal. They could only be who their experience caused them to be. If they never challenged how those experiences changed their lives, they will continue to live according to what they know. It becomes more of a possibility to release the people who hurt us when we understand they only did what they knew and know. It goes hand in hand in releasing pain and releasing those who brought the pain.

Exercise:

Who is the person you are finding the hardest to release?

</br>

What pain inside of you are you struggling to release?

</br>

Do you really want to release it?

What actions are you willing to take in order to begin to release those wounds you have acknowledged and faced?

Breathe...

Actions will determine exactly what you want and what you are ready to remove from your life. Your prayers will begin to change and become more honest when you are ready to release pain, remove the residue and live on the other side of dysfunctional pain. Releasing pain to Jesus is what we must do once the truth of the pain is revealed.

Accepting the truth and walking in it are big steps to take. Truth is a hard pill for many to swallow because we have become so accustomed to dysfunction and walking wounded. To accept the truth of who and where we are is not easy. To accept the truth that our world has been formed on our illusion of love and the hunger for the same, is not easy.

Each day you decide to release the pain and residue of it in your life is a day of overcoming and victory. Each step in your journey of healing is to reclaim the mental, emotional, physical parts of you that have been lost. Choosing to release what no longer serves you creates an area within you to receive what is meant for you to succeed and elevate.

Pain has an end date. How it shows up in your life, has an end date. The amazing thing is that you are the one who can decide today you no longer want to allow the pain of your past to erupt into every area of life and begin to acknowledge, face and release it.

Exercise:

How have you used your pain as an excuse to be negative, bitter, angry or manipulative?

How has your pain blinded you from choosing what is best for you? Ex: because you felt unworthy, you entered and stayed in relationships that are unhealthy

Breathe...

In releasing your pain, it allows your vision and outlook to change. As you release the hold you have on pain and the control pain has on you, it empowers you to choose and do better. It may not be easy to trust your choices, actions or the actions of others in the beginning stages of release, but each day you will be stronger in your belief and trust in yourself.

Begin to declare into your life why you are choosing to release pain, fear, self-doubt, self-sabotage boldly.

Exercise:

I Declare I am releasing _____
because _____

I Declare I am choosing _____
because _____

_____

These simple statements said to yourself daily begin to create a different mindset and understanding of your power that you have always had. Read them out loud daily.

Release comes in thoughts, understanding, and permission. When pain rises up, we can choose to say, "God, thank you for showing me this pain I have been carrying and for showing me I no longer have to carry it alone...I choose to release it to you, now." Simple, honest prayers keep us accountable to ourselves that we are not in denial any longer and are truly desiring a new normal. The desire to be whole has to now be first and foremost.

Masks have been your greatest assets. You learned at pivotal points in your life how to put on the appropriate mask based on who you were around. You learned, as children learn to have an invisible playmate that you pretended to be when you felt that showing up as yourself, would not be acceptable. Your masks begin to crack and reveal the pain behind them as you seek God in truth and desperation for freedom. Your mask allows us to walk around in our lives as strangers to others and ourselves. The more we learn to pretend, the harder it is to accept who is hiding and crouching down behind the mask. As we think about a masquerade ball where everyone is beautifully dressed to a theme designed to hide their true self from those around them, everyone walks around being whatever and whomever they choose to be to be acceptable in the theme of the party. They can be someone else, if only for a few hours. As they connect with people around them, others will try and figure out who they are by their eyes, body language and voice. After a while some may discover who they are behind the mask while others will not take the time to figure it out and simply walk away.

Pretending to be someone you are not in the hopes of acceptance, love and approval is manipulation. Many will walk in and out of your life. Some will take time to get to know the person behind your illusion but many will never take the time to care or look deeper.

In relationships we become who we feel will be accepted by lovers, friends and co-workers. We have believed that our pain and what has happened to us disqualifies us from being acceptable, wanted, needed and mostly, loved. Masks are disguises not only to our physical self, but our emotional, mental and heart self. They are the barriers we use to protect ourselves from additional pain and rejection. In releasing the need or desire to pretend, releasing the pain that impressed upon you that you cannot be enough in being yourself, you can begin to shed the illusion of who you are to yourself. You can release the need to have people in your life who have no desire to look behind your mask and discover your truth.

Exercise:

What mask are you choosing to no longer wear as you release your wounds?

What and Who do you believe your masks protected you from in your life?

What emotions rise up when you think of not using Masks or illusions in your life as you go out into the world?

What are you seeking when you decide to pretend to be something or someone you are not?

Releasing pain is about self honesty. Yes, honesty with self is a valuable gift. The willingness to release what has held you captive requires vulnerability. Releasing what has been your shield, your identity that has left you wondering who you are, is brave. As we are honest with our feelings, our pain, and our fears to God it allows Him to move us into our true identity in Him. Who we are is found in The Father. He says we are brave, strong, wise, appointed, blessed and so much more. Holding on to a false sense of self hinders from receiving the truth about ourselves.

Again, yes you were abandoned, but this is not who you are. Yes, you were abused physically, but this is not who you are. Yes, you believed in those who did not show themselves trustworthy or worthy of your time, but this is not who you are. Yes, you didn't finish your degree, but this does not define you. As we make room for truth, we make room for healing.

Exercise

Where in your life do you need to be honest with yourself?

What unfulfilled expectation in others or yourself are you ready to release?

Breathe...

Having expectations in others who don't have the capacity to fulfill them sets you up for disappointment. Many times, those whom we are expecting to come through for us, do not know we are expecting them to do something or be something in our lives. Attempting to validate ourselves by accomplishments, thinking they will bring affirmation, approval, likes, love or something else we may need, only sets us up for disappointment.

Your journey towards healing requires you to begin to drop the expectations at the door and walk over them. Those you feel let you down because they were not able to give you what you needed must be released from your disappointment. You must release yourself from the need to receive affirmation and approval from completing something, being something, that others would acknowledge.

Free yourself as you walk over what you have let go of and refuse to pick it back up. You risk never being able to see your true potential and ability by living life on what you feel others expect from you. Free yourself from the prison of expectation. Unshackle your heart, mind, spirit, soul, feet, hands from the expectations in what could not love you, could not build you, could not affirm you and did not fulfill you but left you searching for more. You hold the key to the doors of the prisons that you have lived in. Free Yourself.

Mirror Work:

Look into your eyes, not just at your face. Look in your mirror and say (your name) _____ I am accepted in God and He fulfills every expectation and His love is enough for me.

Exercise:

Clear The Space

You have done lots of work today. Go back to your list of the people and the things you need to release. Grab a piece of paper and write those names and things down in ink. Why in ink? Because it is permanent. Set the timer for 5 minutes and write who and what comes to your mind as you may realize or you have been holding on to more than you actually are aware. Once you are done, ball it up and burn it. As these expectations, pain, wounds, fear and what represents the people who hurt you, disappointed you or walked away begin to burn, you are burning away what is attached to them within you. This is symbolic of laying these wounds at the feet of Jesus and allowing the blood of Jesus to remove them. Pray, worship, pray and worship some more. What you have laid at the feet of the alter, leave it there and walk away in your mind, your body, your spirit and heart. Declare your freedom.

When you are done, document it here:

I cleaned _____ on _____, 20 ____ and I feel

Breathe...

The next step is permission.

I give myself permission to _____ at this stage of my journey:

In the space below write a letter to yourself about what you are going to give yourself permission to do regarding releasing your pain to Jesus. How will your life be different by giving yourself permission to walk away from the things, thoughts and people who hurt, betrayed or abused you?

Example: I give myself permission to believe that what I have released to God, I am free from now, in Jesus' name, Amen. I release anything I expected to fulfill me, affirm me or approve me.

Breathe...

Affirmation: I Am free from the shackles of the pain and people who hurt me.

Prayer:

God, thank you for giving me the courage to release my pain, the residue of my pain and the people I entrusted my heart to whether knowingly or unknowingly. I thank you that as I am true to myself and pray honest prayers to share my heart with you, I am grateful I can daily walk out my freedom in Jesus name, Amen

NOTES:

Chapter 7:

Learning to Forgive Others

This step can be hard. Sometimes my hurt seemed so deep that I could not conceive forgiving anyone that caused it. In some ways, I came to the false conclusion that by holding on to what someone did to me, I was hurting them in some way. I did not understand that by not forgiving I was locked into the pain and remained at the point of the hurt.

Exercise...

What is your understanding of forgiveness?

How does your understanding of forgiveness coincide with God's Truth of forgiveness?

We are wanting to first and foremost identify our understanding of forgiveness because it will determine how well you are able to work through this process. According to ww.psychcentral.com, **forgiveness is letting go of the need for revenge and releasing negative thoughts of bitterness and resentment.** As in all steps in the journey of healing, understanding what our belief and knowledge of forgiveness, determines how we go through this process. Remember the process? Process is the action of going forward. In order to go forward, we must be willing to not skip steps but boldly take the next step knowing it is rebuilding your foundation. Many times, we want to skip the step of forgiveness because we can see it as letting someone off the hook and we feel they need to stay on the hook for a lifetime.

I have learned forgiveness is a powerful release to the one forgiving. Choosing not to forgive is bondage to the one holding the grudge. Forgiveness, for me, sounded like another way for those who hurt me to win over me.

Exercise:

When thinking of forgiveness, what emotions rise up in your heart, mind, memory?

Breathe...

As we live life striving to outlive the trauma we have experienced, we can begin to cover the pain with anger and bitterness and live in a state of defense. These emotions become our shields. To consider forgiveness as an option shifts our position from being in control to be being vulnerable. This can make you question if you are really ready to release everything that has held you hostage since your childhood. Peace can only come by releasing your anger and hurt and beginning to forgive.

Exercise:

What is the hardest part about forgiveness for you?

```
┌─────────────────────────────────────┐
│                                     │
│                                     │
│                                     │
│                                     │
└─────────────────────────────────────┘
```

Who are you resistant to forgive? List the names below…

```
┌─────────────────────────────────────┐
│                                     │
│                                     │
│                                     │
│                                     │
└─────────────────────────────────────┘
```

Why are you resistant to forgive them? Be Totally Honest

What does forgiving those you have listed, mean to you?

Breathe...

Many times, we are told to forgive, but it is told to us as if we are to do this immediately. I learned through my journey that again, this is a process. It is a process that comes along with:

1. acknowledging hurt
2. facing hurt
3. releasing hurt

4. accepting what we have endured
5. accepting who has hurt us
6. understanding our feelings about it.

We can get stuck in the different steps along the way, if we are not careful. We can get stuck when others devalue our pain or ignore it. We can feel that we must ignore what we have gone through sometimes because it is easier to ignore it than face it and acknowledge it. In each stage of the process of forgiveness, we must allow yourself to feel the emotions that comes along with it. Otherwise, we risk getting lost and stuck in the steps and end up creating a deeper well of pain attached to the wound that is already deep. I also learned that forgiveness is a heart issue. Yes, a heart issue.

Forgiveness happens when we allow our heart to shift from all the emotions attached to what we have endured no longer is worth holding on to. We can scream and yell that we forgive someone, but our actions and responses to them, tell the real story. We don't want to say we forgive someone as simply mouth service when our heart is still intertwined with the act and emotion of what we have endured.

Forgiveness can come in stages. I learned that as God brings different things to remembrance as we go through healing, we must choose to forgive and work the process again to shift our heart in the season we are in. When pain goes deep, so does unforgiveness. You don't want a false sense of forgiveness in your heart because again, you are only hurting yourself. Forgiveness is never about the other person, it is for you. It sets you free. Others may not understand why you have forgiven, but again, it is not for anyone else, just you.

Exercise:

Have you said you have forgiven someone and yet when you heard their name or saw them, the same rage, fear etc. rose up inside you? What did you do?

Is your heart still holding on to negative emotions towards the person (s) who caused you pain? Do you want to let it go or does it serve you in some way?

What is the hardest part for you in releasing this person(s) and the negative emotions attached to it

Breathe...

You will know when you have forgiven. You will feel it in your spirit, your mind and mostly in your heart. Just as we receive God, Love, His forgiveness in our heart, we will feel the same release in every part of us. As we think back over where we have come through and the people who helped to bring pain into our lives, we will begin to recognize if we are still moving in anger/resentment or if when those memories come, there is a peace within. If there is anything other than that, there is still work to do and only you can do it.

For many years, I believed I had forgiven so many. Yet, when I heard their names or someone would bring them up in conversation, my body language changed, and I felt a twinge of anger and even sometimes rage. God showed me, I had said the words, "I forgive them," but in my heart I was still holding on to what they did to me, how I felt as a result of it, and the resentment that it was done. Forgiveness begins in the spirit as we accept that God has forgiven us and has instructed us to forgive others. The soul, to me, reminds me of a Disney movie where you are in a circle and all of your life journeys and experiences are swirling around you. This vision brings some joy and mostly pain as you begin to reflect on all you have been through. There is a process to forgive. Each time there is an offense, the process must begin again. Forgiveness cannot merely be a script of words because the Bible tells you to do so. If those words are not attached to a heart, mind and spirit that have embraced forgiveness, there is a disconnect.

The steps to forgive:

1. Acknowledge the act/word
2. Acknowledge the pain it brought
3. Acknowledge the person who caused it and the impact of it

4. Deal with the results of the offense (anger, fear, distrust, betrayal, etc.)
5. Deal with how the results of the offense changed your life
6. Deal with the emotions and mindset shifts the offenses caused (good & bad)
7. Give yourself permission to Release the offense, the emotions and the desire to hold on to baggage of the offense
8. Choose to release the person who brought the offense and allow your heart to Forgive them
9. Choose to forgive yourself for your part in the cycle of unforgiveness.
10. Give yourself permission (authority) to release everything attached to offense and emotions it brought
11. 11 Change your words about the person and the situations
12. 12 Allow God to clean up any residue in your Mind, Heart, Soul, Spirit

As you can see, this process takes time. You may find yourself staying on some steps more than others, depending on how deep the pain is, how long you have held it, and the person who offended or hurt you. I have had to add to these steps as I have gone through the healing process, but to me it only strengthens me by making sure I am free from anything that hinders me from being my best.

Exercise:

In the steps above, which one (s) seems to be the hardest for you to accept and do?

```
┌─────────────────────────────────────────┐
│                                         │
│                                         │
│                                         │
│                                         │
└─────────────────────────────────────────┘
```

Why is this step (s) difficult for you?

```
┌─────────────────────────────────────────┐
│                                         │
│                                         │
│                                         │
│                                         │
└─────────────────────────────────────────┘
```

What emotions come to you when considering starting or completing the journey of forgiveness?

[ ]

Is the thought of forgiveness harder because of the act done or the person who caused the hurt/offense?

[ ]

Do you believe it is beneficial to you to forgive? Why or Why not

[ ]

Breathe…

The acts done to us, whether in words or actions, silenced us. They stole our voice and our ability to say no. Yet, through forgiveness we regain it all. It is a power move. It is a self-care move. It is a huge part of healing. Again, this part of the process will not only bring up the pain but the rage and fear attached to it. With each pull of the rope and each step taken on the stairs, you regain inner power, your inner voice and the noose around your wrist, feet and hands, fall to the floor.

Mirror Work:

Look into your eyes, not just at your face. Look in your mirror and say (your name) _____ I choose to release those who have taken up residence in my mind, heart, spirit and soul through unforgiveness. I choose to forgive them and their acts as an act of self-love, Amen

You just began the process to unshackle your hands and feet from the pain that brought you to this place of unforgiveness. Your heart can beat differently. Your vision can be clearer for your life. Whenever you feel that anger is rebuilding in you as the memories fade into your mind, go back to your mirror and make your declaration again.

How does it feel looking into your eyes and saying this affirmation to yourself?

```
┌─────────────────────────────────────────┐
│                                         │
│                                         │
│                                         │
│                                         │
│                                         │
│                                         │
└─────────────────────────────────────────┘
```

Breathe...

Exercise:

Clear The Space

You have done lots of work today. Now it is time to symbolically clean your natural space as you are cleaning inner space. Many times, we have something that reminds us of painful moments in our past. It can be a piece of clothing, a piece of jewelry, something written, a picture, etc. Today you are going to set your timer for 10 minutes and go to the place where you are holding these memoirs and throw them out of your house. You can burn them or put them all in a bag and throw it away outside your home. In doing so, you are doing a natural act of releasing and letting go. You cannot move forward when you have a lot of old things hanging around. The physical act is symbolizing the work you are doing in your heart, mind and soul.

When you are done, document it here:

I cleaned _____ on _____, 20 ____ and I feel

The next step is permission. As you uncover parts of yourself that have been hidden, you must give yourself permission to acknowledge, face and deal with what you find. Please complete the Permission Exercise Below.

I give myself permission to: _____ at this stage of my journey:

In the space below write a letter to yourself about what you are going to give yourself permission to do regarding forgiving others and releasing them. How will your life be different by giving yourself permission to allow Gods' love to replace the areas in your life where unforgiveness dwells.

Example: I give myself permission to acknowledge who hurt or betrayed me and the emotions I feel because of it. I give myself permission to no longer allow those acts to control me in any way and I give myself permission to allow God to fill those empty places with Him.

Breathe…

Affirmation: I am forgiven, therefore, I choose to forgive.

Prayer:

God, thank you for forgiving me and giving me the courage to release the pain of my past through forgiveness. I now understand that holding on to the people and the acts done to me in unforgiveness, serves me no purpose. Thank you, God, for giving me the strength to lay down my sword of anger and unforgiveness and pick up your Word.

NOTES:

Chapter 8:

Choosing To Forgive Yourself

You have arrived at a pivotal moment. A transforming moment. This is by far my hardest obstacle. Forgiving others takes time. However, forgiving yourself was unheard of for me. I didn't realize that finding myself would require me to dig so deep within. As I began to really look at who I was, I began to feel a lot of guilt about my decisions in my relationships, my decisions in how I lived my life and wondering why I made some of them.

Those choices caused so much pain for me, and it was embarrassing. As parts of my life replayed in my heart, mind and soul the guilt of my decisions was in the forefront of my life.

The same steps that it takes to forgive others also need to be taken to forgive ourselves. Often times the steps to forgiving oneself are even greater because it requires self-inventory.

Self- Inventory can become an activity of self judgement if we are not careful.

Exercise:

When you think of doing self-inventory, what thoughts come to mind?

```
┌─────────────────────────────────────┐
│                                     │
│                                     │
│                                     │
│                                     │
└─────────────────────────────────────┘
```

Take each of those thoughts and write down what they are attached to?

```
┌─────────────────────────────────────┐
│                                     │
│                                     │
│                                     │
│                                     │
└─────────────────────────────────────┘
```

When I made the decision to do whatever I had to do as a child to get love, I made the decision from a desperate and fearful place. It was sheer desperation to feel wanted, appreciated and loved. This decision, as I spoke of earlier, caused a lifetime of pain. Yet when I wanted to discover why all my relationships with men were the same, the root of my choice had to be acknowledged. I needed to take responsibility for my choices. The truth that I needed to forgive myself for not knowing any better became clear.

Exercise:

Choices? What choices have you made in relationships that are directly related to insecurity, unworthiness, feeling unloved, or feeling abandoned?

When choosing relationships, Intimate and otherwise, how did your past wounds push you into desperation when making a choice to stay or leave?

Breathe...

The way I acknowledge what others had done to me was the way I needed to acknowledge what I had done to myself through desperation. The guilt was eating me up inside and bringing anger with it. By being honest with myself I understood that I was holding myself bound by the past. The chains around my neck were held by those I hadn't forgiven, including myself. It was not my fault that others didn't know how to love me. However; it was my fault that I taught people how to treat me in my desperation. I showed men I was insecure by shutting down my voice to allow theirs to be heard. I showed them I would accept whatever they gave me by accepting their excuses of why they never had time for me. I assured them I was not going anywhere when somehow, I became a victim when they cheated, and I felt it was because I was not good enough. I had to learn to forgive me for what I didn't know or understand and for what I chose. Choosing is powerful. It is a gift and a curse, sometimes. By choosing to search for love, this choice brought pain because I searched outside of God and myself. I chose to stay where I was tolerated and not wanted. This choice allowed my self- esteem, my self-worth, my voice, my mind and more to be tainted. In turn, I was a victim of my choices and the results of them.

Yet, when I chose to accept that my identity is in God and not my pain, people or the results of my past, my choice became a gift. When I chose to accept I no longer needed to be a victim, choice became a gift for me. When I chose to forgive myself for my part in my hurt, my choice allowed me freedom. It is not an easy decision, but a necessary one. The ability to look at yourself and actually see who you are and choose to forgive yourself is powerful and bold. Life will happen and each time we are able to pick ourselves up, and by choosing to forgive ourselves we give ourselves permission to heal and grow.

Exercise:

Where are you feeling stuck in your life, because you haven't forgiven yourself?

What is the reason you feel you cannot forgive yourself for your choices?

Do you see yourself as unforgiveable and if so, why?

By forgiving yourself, you open doors to your life you didn't know were possible. Does knowing this give you the courage to let go? Why or Why not?

Breathe...

Self Forgiveness released me from the shame that some of my choices brought. It can release you also if you are willing. It is a genuine love for self. It allows you to unshackle yourself from lies and come face to face with the truth. It gives you the courage to say, "Yes that is who I was and that is what I did, but it is not who I was birthed to become."

Forgiveness is transforming. When God forgave our sin it allowed us to move from slavery and bondage to freedom and deliverance. By choosing to forgive ourselves we step out of chains into a crown of glory.

Exercise:

Have you accepted that God has forgiven you for everything you have done?

Do you believe there is sin in your life and your past that God could never forgive you for? If yes, is this the reason you struggle to forgive yourself?

Breathe…

I never knew all these years that I was holding myself captive. I blamed everyone else for all my pain and hardship. Yes, there were others responsible, but in order to find my true self I needed to own my truth. Owning my truth opened the door that says my captivity as well as my freedom was in my hands. I realized that I had become comfortable in my pain because it was all I knew. Forgiving myself says that I can have a new comfort. I chose to receive the comfort and love that came with releasing myself from my own prison and walking in freedom. Each time I remembered something and dealt with everything that came with it, I chose to forgive me because I knew the freedom it would give. I believe the greatest gift is loving myself for who I am with all my flaws. The love that God gives me allows me to embrace my flaws and still love me.

God knew I was flawed and He sent His Son Jesus to cover my sins through His blood and wash me clean (Matthew 1:21, Revelation 1:5)

Exercise…

Are you really ready to let go of self embraced mental and emotional prisons you are in because you refuse to forgive yourself?

What are the steps you are ready to take to begin the process of forgiveness toward you?

Remember the steps to forgiveness apply to you also…

The steps to forgive:

1. Acknowledge the act/word
2. Acknowledge the pain it brought
3. Acknowledge the person who caused it and the impact of it
4. Deal with the results of the offense (anger, fear, distrust, betrayal, etc.)
5. Deal with how the results of the offense changed your life

6. Deal with the emotions and mindset shifts the offenses caused (good & bad)
7. Give yourself permission to Release the offense, the emotions and the desire to hold on to baggage of the offense
8. Choose to release the person who brought the offense and allow your heart to Forgive them
9. Choose to forgive yourself for your part in the cycle of unforgiveness.
10. Give yourself permission (authority) to release everything attached to offense and emotions it brought
11. 11 Change your words about the person and the situations
12. 12 Allow God to clean up any residue in your Mind, Heart, Soul, Spirit

Which step are you willing to start today to forgive yourself? Why?

Based on what you have done since first stating what is the hardest part about self forgiveness for you in the beginning? What is the hardest step in forgiveness for you now? What is the struggle with it?

What work are you willing to do in order to overcome the struggle of letting go and freeing yourself from unforgiveness?

Breathe...

Remember this, God has forgiven you. The Creator of the world has sent His son to die for all you have done and will ever think to do. He forgave you and He loves you so unconditionally. Don't become your own God of judgement by refusing to FORGIVE YOU. Use your power of choice to break the self-inflicted chains on your mind, emotions, feet, hands, heart and your life. You didn't deserve to be forgiven, but through God's love, grace and mercy, He chose to. Now it is your turn to do the same. You owe it to yourself.

Exercise:

Clear The Space

You have done lots of work today. Now it is time to symbolically clean your natural space as you are cleaning inner space. Create a safe space in your home, closet, car or go to a park. Light a few candles. Take your journal and pen. Turn on your choice of music that allows you to be reflective and puts you in a mindset of peace. Allow yourself to drift away from everything that is requiring your time and just be with God. Allow yourself the freedom to just be in the moment. Begin to write in your journal the thoughts and emotions that arise in this sacred space and allow the tears to flow without judgement. As you are writing, you are clearing your inner space of the words, memories and the residue of self sabotage and making room for God's grace and mercy to flow into them. Release yourself from the bondage of the past and the unforgiveness of self that lies there. Stay in that sacred place as long as you are able and then get up, dust yourself off with your hands from the top of your head down to your feet. To me this is symbolic of shaking off the dust and becoming clean. I'm so proud of you.

When you are done, document it here:

I cleaned _____ on _____, 20 ____ and I feel

The next step is permission. As you uncover parts of yourself that have been hidden, you must give yourself permission to acknowledge, face and deal with what you find. Please complete the Permission Exercise Below.

I give myself permission to: _____ at this stage of my journey:

In the space below write a letter to yourself about what you are going to give yourself permission to do regarding forgiving others and releasing them. How will your life be different by giving yourself permission to allow Gods' love to replace the areas in your life where unforgiveness dwells?

Example: I give myself permission to forgive myself for _____ and release it to God.

Breathe...

Affirmation: I Am forgiven and I choose to forgive myself. I am worth it.

Prayer:

God, thank you for forgiving me and giving me the courage to forgive myself. Thank you for helping me to see that by forgiving myself, I am freeing myself and releasing the hold of the past in my life. I am grateful that you love me so much. I am grateful that even though I have seen myself as flawed, you see me as more and I thank you. In Jesus name, Amen

NOTES:

Conclusion:

As you come to the end of this workbook, I want to applaud you.

As you have gone through the exercises and the information and you didn't finish or skipped some of them, it's totally expected and understood. As you go through your journey of healing, know it is not a race. It is a journey of life, but I do want you to applaud yourself for making the effort, doing the work and choosing to not be a victim, and choosing to discover your truth of who you are. Applaud yourself for doing the work to break free from the situations that have stopped you from knowing your voice, knowing that you are loved and loving others authentically.

As time goes on and when you are ready, go back to the questions that were too hard to answer because of the emotions they brought up or the feelings you have to the right answers. Go back, when you are ready to read and complete them. Allow yourself the opportunity to dig deeper. Please remember as you go through this process, today, tomorrow or next year, give yourself the permission to reach out for the help you may need. If you feel that this journey is too hard to go at alone, reach out to those can assist you. A psychologist, physician or counselor to assist you in working through this process and help you make sense of what you are discovering and uncovering is a great asset to your journey.

No matter what, don't give up on you. Don't give up on the process of healing. Don't give up on yourself when the times seem hard. Trust the plan God has for you. Trust the process and know you are not alone.

You have come to the end of this workbook, but you have not come to the end of your story. Keep giving yourself permission to turn the page. Continue to give yourself permission to add new pages to your story, ones of victory, overcoming, and finding out each day more of who you are underneath, pain, shame and silence.

Trust yourself through the process by making a decision and following through to complete what you start, to be honest with your answers and to know that you are enough, and you are deserving to walk and live your REAL SELF.

Until we meet again, God Bless you, God Bless you.

Lynette M Bradshaw

About the Author

Lynette M Bradshaw began writing many years ago for her former church as she discovered her gift of writing through God's leading. It wasn't until many years later, she began to write for herself as a way of dealing with heartache in her search for love and acceptance and the desire to heal her negative view of Self. Lynette is also the author of, In Search of Me-The Workbook, Moments of Gratitude Journal (Companion Journal for In Search of Me) The Locked Chamber: Healing The Hearts of God's Daughters. She is a Transformational Speaker, Coach & Photographer. She is a graduate of Louisiana Business college and Medvance Institute and currently works in the medical field as a Medical Assistant.

When she is not writing, she can be found enjoying photography, spending time with her children, dancing and exercising.

Pick up a copy In Search of Me: A Journey to Self-Love, Self-Worth & Purpose and Moments of Gratitude-Journal at www.Amazon.com or www.RestoreHerWorth.com

Contact Information

Website: www.RestoreHerWorth.com

Facebook: http://bit.ly/LynetteMBradshaw

YouTube:

https://tinyurl.com/LynetteMBradshawLive

www.ingramcontent.com/pod-product-compliance
Lightning Source LLC
Chambersburg PA
CBHW071006160426
43193CB00012B/1939